Geordie La Cosa Nostra
{This thing of ours}

An Anthology of Gangster chic and "Faces" in the NorthEast

Prologue

La Geordie Cosa Nostra

This Thing of Ours

This one off book is a rare insight into the true world of the most elite Gangsters and hard men or as they prefer to be known "*Faces*" in the North East

Chapters

Chapter One……………………..My Life
Chapter Two…………...…………..Geordie Topham
Chapter Three…………………...…...."Big" Billy Robinson
Chapter Four…………………Lenny "The Guvner" Mclean
Chapter Five…………………………..Ernie Bewick
Chapter Six……………………….....Liddle Towers
Chapter Seven……………………...The Sayers Family
Chapter Eight………………………….Paddy Conroy
Chapter Nine…………………………..Michael Bulloch
Chapter Ten……………………………Ian Freeman
Chapter Eleven………………………...Viv Graham
Chapter Twelve………………………...Raoul Moat
Chapter Thirteen……………..………..John Mario Cummings
Chapter Fourteen……………..………..Davey Falcus
Chapter Fifteen…………………………Geoffrey Harrison
Chapter Sixteen………………..………Brian Cockrill
Chapter Seventeen…………………....…Lee Duffy

Finally…………………………………………………………………..

Chapter One

La cosa nostra is an Italian term and it literally translates to

"this thing of ours"

It's also a common term used to address the Italian/American Dons with a direct ascendancy and blood line to Sicily who are allegedly involved in organized crime, also termed The Mob, The Mafioso, or Mafia

When I got the feeling that one more idiot pointing one more shooter at my canister is just one gun to much, it's time for a re-think, so Gateshead or Italy, well that's a no brainer.

So

In the words of Dave Courtney,

the world's hardest working celebrity

gangster

"stop the world, I want to get off"

I did exactly that, I got off, did I see enough, do enough and batter enough people, oh fuck me yes, so I'm off to get some 50-degree sun on my old bones, and write my book whilst sitting beside my pool drinking something long and cold.

Living in the North East of England in the height of the Gangster Chic period I have some stories and a rich vein of colorful characters to talk about, some of the plastic gangsters and pseudo plastic "gangbangers" are more talk than walk, but trust me on this, the North East has bred some double hard, snot and blood on the cobble bastards.?

One or two of the people I speak about in my book have been spoken about before in other books, and even as the "stars" of TV shows, sometimes good, sometimes just shite, rubbish and lies, but in this book I will give you an intimate insight to some men who I hold a great reverence and respect for, do they deserve this respect?, in my world and their world they do, no thieves, no drug dealers, just proper "stand up, top boys" who can have a row, knock you the fuck out, and there is no hard feelings.

Who I am, well there is an old saying, the best trick the devil ever pulled was convincing the world he didn't exist.

If I want you to know who I am,

you *already know*

I will say this, the best of what can be termed successful gangbangers are hardly noticeable, they are inconspicuous grey men who almost seem to be no more than on the periphery of crime and criminals, but this is intentional, trust me, these are the men that pull the strings and have the big pay day, these men are geniuses by anyone's standards. In every occasion when you think that you know that hardest of top boys in your town, you don't, you know a sergeant at best, and he will answer to someone higher in the tree

A quote from John "Mario" Cummings, the most famous of the notorious "Geordie Mafia"

"Only losers spend 10 or 20 years in jail, the real villains, the men with style, cunning and intelligence don't get caught"

I never had any time to sit around bars with other wide boys telling fucking big lies about what I've done, what I've robbed, or who I could batter, no, I have always been intensely interested in a pocket full of cabbage (cash) and making my pile bigger.

But "*the life*" is a gamble, and the harder you play the bigger you lose, true most of the time you will win but when you lose, and you always lose at some point, your life and liberty is gone, no home, no woman, no family, fuck all, you're on your own or worse in a cell with an arsehole who's feet stink, with shite food on plastic plates, a T-shirt with HMP printed on it and, unless you can fight, the risk of getting done up the arse, dry!

My interests spanned all of the northeast, name a nefarious trade and I have wrung the last copper coin out of it, If I wanted something and couldn't afford it, fuck it, I simply took it, the civilians call me a horrible cunt, the proper people in my life,

the people who I like,

like me,

The chaps I speak about in this book will know who I am, that's enough said.

So as an old man do I want to disappear now and stay under the radar, living in the sun, with all the trappings,

You can bet your bollocks I do

I turned out the way I have because I guess I was always destined to be, and I don't kid myself in any way when I say this because I am intelligent enough to know what I am, and to embrace what I am, a text book sociopath (no conscience) and a fucking greedy magpie, if its shiny and it's not mine, I want it, I don't know why I want it, I can't help it, I just gotta have it.

As a chavi I never had any emotional or other problems, my

mam and dad remained in a happy marriage all of their lives, they gave me everything, I could ever want, they didn't drink, they didn't fight, or argue, and surprisingly given how I topped up, they were very quiet gentle nurturing folk who never hurt a fly, and our home was always clean and well kept. My life as a kid was idyllic. I lived in the same house all of my childhood, I was a grammar school boy, so what the fuck went wrong with me? well that's simple, I like violence, I like to talk about it, I like to watch it, it's almost a primeval urge, I am drawn to it like a moth to a flame, it's the same with violent people, I find it easy to relate to people like me, violent loud people, and if we hurt each other along the way, who cares, it was laughed off.

So this is my comfort zone, it is as simple as that, some twelve-year-old quack with a psychiatry degree might spout the latest fashionable psychobabble and tell me shite about not being breast fed and starved of affection or some other shite, this is rubbish, absolute nonsense, I was good at what I did and

I just fucking loved the life I have led. but note the past tense, *loved*.

My adult life was a bit of a paradox on one hand living in a world of top drawer villains and gangsters, and on the other mixing with the Lords, Earls and other landed gentry on their private estates in Durham and Northumberland engaged in my favorite pastimes, shooting and other country pursuits, these estates are millionaires playgrounds, but let me differentiate between millionaires and people with serious wealth, multi-millionaires, people this wealthy are hardly seen, except when they want to be of course, they only mix with other multi-millionaires, and rarely outside of their *VERY* select circles.

So the players in my world? they show their wealth with ostentation, sometimes brashly, with the latest model of Range Rover, may be a Bayliner *blue sea* boat in Puerto Banus, and the " *right*" model of Rolex watch, I have all the usual toys, but what made it easy for me to integrate into this society was my Grammar school background, this gave me access to elite circles and the company of millionaires, this kind of life, on an almost daily basis fueled my thirst for " more" of everything,

I have always been curious as to why celebritics and *uber* wealthy people are attracted to hard men and gangsters, who knows but I fitted in with the country set with consummate ease, however the thug life was also mine, it suited me, but it suits very few people, and here is the rub, there is a huge cost, because of the way I have led my life I have lost family, I have lost friends, but the most valuable thing to lose is time, and let me make something very plain at this point, and this might surprise you when I say this but, for as much as I have laughed my ass off throughout my life, the truth is I'm a mug, for every minute I have spent in a police or jail cell, I'm a prize fucking idiot, I could have gangbanged until the day I die but the time I have wasted locked up is gone for good, forever, and the reality is this, you can buy anything you want, if you have enough cash, but, you cannot buy time, imagine you are on your death bed, at your last gasp, how much would you pay for one more healthy day?, or being able to laugh your arse off one time, or one last shag !, imagine that, how much would you pay?

your answer?

I bet that it's the same as my answer, and it is this, you would pay EVERYTHING, including your last copper coin and BOTH of your bollocks. So time? in my experience it is the one thing that cannot be bought or stolen, trust me, no matter how clever you think you are, the biggest gang in the UK can beat you, and they all have the first name, PC............

My introduction to the life was, I guess with my Granddad, he was 6`7, Irish, my Mothers dad, half or part Irish Gipsy, part northeast `pitman` a fucking true monster of a man in every way.

{I won't say his name as it is the same as mine, and although I am definitely the `black sheep` of my family, and truthfully I see the other men in my family as pretty much "fannies" but I still respect their privacy, I respect the fact that La Cosa Nostra is my life and is definitely not, nor should it ever be theirs

My Grandads version of right and wrong, good and bad was blurred at best, his idea of quality time was to show me how to fight, better yet, street fight, to him this was just good wholesome fun.

I remember when I was maybe six or seven and at the "Hoppings" with my Grandad {the Hoppings was a large traveler fair held in Newcastle} and at that time it was still PC to have boxing booths, my granddad used to love this, it was nothing but a challenge, so here we were in a tent with hundreds of people and a boxing ring, the challenge was, if you could survive three rounds you won £5, a white fiver. I remember the boxer was a really big mush and as hairy as a bear.

So Grandad decides it's his turn, all his pals were egging him on so he say's had on t' me jacket and collar son", he paid his half crown and in the ring he climbs, as I said he was nearly a giant to most men, but the boxer was also a big lump, so the bell rings and the big hairy mush comes out swinging and he connects with Grandad on the jaw, the crowd think that's it, lights out, but my old granddad says , if that's arl yuv got son yer in trouble now, and he launched a straight right into the middle of the sasquatches chest, old hairy went down onto one knee, and I remember looking at this fucking huge sweaty bear on his knees, gasping for breath, head down and a thin line of snot slowly dribbling out of his nose.

My granddads pals went berserk, they even started to count, one, two, three, I got passed into the ring and granddad lifted my up on his shoulder, by this time the count was at eight, nine, ten DING DING DING, and it's all over, the owner came over to granddad and offered him the fiver, but winning wasn't good enough, he wanted round two and he say's "why nor son a haven't broken a sweat yet, get your boy up and have double or quits", but old hairy wanted none of it, so granddad says, give the fiver to the boy, so there I was at the Hoppings with a white fiver a huge amount at that time most people had never even seen a £5 note but that was my old Grandad, and my first gangster lesson, easy come easy go.

My life, it has been like this for the last 50 years, cars,

houses, police, cash, violence, this was the life, nothing was too expensive and no one was a barrier, me and my pals were adhesive and would give each other anything, because the truth of it is, for most people in "the life" this is their family, so now? here I am an old gang banger sitting beside my pool at my villa in the sun, with all the trappings, I stopped the world and I got off, I left the life for good, will it leave me, ? who knows, I hope so, but that's easy to say when you have a few quid and most people would say you have the life of a king, so take a picture of me here today and what do you see ?, let me tell you You will see the opening scene from the film Sexy Beast the one where retired London gangster Ray Winston is lying on a sun lounger with his gut out, in 50-degree sun, brown and sweaty, and he growls

"I`m sweatin here, roastin"

only with me, it's not a film.

I was

THE LIFE

Chapter

2

George "Geordie" Topham

George
"Geordie"
Topham
{In fancy dress}

North of the Tyne "Geordie" Topham might not be well known, it just wasn't his turf, but in Durham and Wearside, on his turf, he was the "capo de capo", DA KING, he was a huge 30 stone mountain of a man from the Houghton area, and the spitting image of Jackie Gleeson {the actor}, how this man was never a millionaire I just don't know, but he was always as poor as a church mouse, when I think back to this time in the early eighties, we all had the toys, Porsche 911's or at least 924's, they were easy to get, if you could have a row, you worked on the doors and as security at the rave scene, a grand a week was about what we earned, not for Geordie though, he drove a red Tranny van, what the fuck!, but never the less, he was a top drawer dealer in violence.

His connections were in the traveler community, mostly Irish travelers, horses, gold debt collection, they were his stock in trade, debt collection was never about menacing poor folks who just couldn't pay, what was the point?, no it was collecting "un-collectable" debts from prize shithouses who could pay but just wouldn't, I never saw him go all in, gob and baseball bat, his way was quiet at first and then if the mug still wouldn't cough up, he just launched them about the house until they were a little more forthcoming !

I kid you not I once saw Geordie go into a punters gaff to collect a gambling debt, the kid had nothing, he had pissed the lot, so to prove a point Geordie took all the furniture including the dinner table WITH THE PLATES OF DINNER STILL ON IT! I laughed so hard the tears were running down my face, he just couldn't see why it was so funny, until I told him, as I was walking out of the gaff the mug asked if he could have his curry back!

The time I spent with big Geordie Topham was fucking hilarious, he was the mutts nuts to be teamed up with, every day was a proper laugh, but never was I far away from proper violence, it was Geordie who introduced me into the world of Gipsy bare knuckle fighting, I remember once he said, "look we have to gan 't' Ireland to see Michael Cash fight". So off we went, across the country to Liverpool and got the ferry to Belfast, IN THE 70'S, you might not know this but going to Ireland at that time with English accents and in an English van, was just stupid, we might as well have put a big target on our arses, we must have been mad, no deranged !, anyway we got to the town {crossmaglen} and the whole town was heaving with travelers to see this brawl, the other kid {a mush called Joyce} was already here in the center of the village, but Michael Cash was nowhere to be seen, after two fucking hours an old merc turned up and there is Cash with his entourage, about four or five lumps.

After a bit of shouting and shoving The mush called Joyce decided it was the wrong day, the crowd went berserk, a few small fights broke out and the Gipsy who organized the *pagger* Bartley Gorman somehow managed to calm the crowd down, so for a few minutes everything seemed ok and I started to foolishly think I might get home without a shiv in me, or so I thought

Then there was the very loud noise of an army helicopter overhead, Geordie said "listen son, if this chopper lands keep yer hands where they can be seen, and don't do anything to spook these army boys they are just kids with big fuck off guns and every day they wake up thinking is today the day some paddy shoots the back of my knees out, oh and the gipsy boys will be strapped as well" I was about fifteen at the time, so after I had shit myself and cried for me Mam a bit , I decided to do the statue thing and not move, so the chopper lands and about 20 camouflaged kids jump out, what they thought they were going to do with about 500 Gipsy lumps that were pissed up and probably strapped {carrying a tool} but they had a wander round, asked if it was a grudge match, and then climbed back in and took off, what the fuck? I just wanted to go home, double fast!

Geordie died about 2004, my mucker Stu told me, sadly I had not seen George for about 20 years, he must have been about 70 I guess, but I got the details and went to Durham crematorium, I thought I was going to be like Ronnie and Reggie's send off, may be with Dave Courtney running things in a full length mohair Crombie, no! about ten people turned up to see this legend off, it later transpired that he had been dead for three days before anyone found him, he was living on his own in a caravan on a fucking allotment, how could that happen, he was known up and down the country,

A sad end to a massive character, well not really, pissing around in the 80's me and Geordie had sheds full of fun, truthfully, I don't think he would have changed his life one bit, a character? a "face?", yes, a grand master.

I haven't forgotten you mate.

Chapter

3
"BIG" BILLY ROBINSON
Gateshead

There cannot be many people in the Northeast underworld or even the whole of the UK who will have a bad word said against Big Billy Robinson, even teams and families that are traditionally pitted against each other with infamous names like "Sayers" "Richardson" or "Conroy" will all say the same thing, Big Billy Robinson is one of the greatest street fighters the Northeast has ever seen, each and every one to a man, not one bad word!

I was once in Lewisham (London) with a pal and I was coincidently talking to Lenny Mclean (bare knuckle boxer and famed Barry the Baptist in the film, Lock stock and two smoking barrels) and although they had never met, this man had nothing but admiration and respect for " Big" Billy Robinson.

I have known Big Billy for a long time, he has even looked after a couple of my bars for me and one thing that always impressed me is this, he is the only man I have ever met that is incapable of telling a lie, that may sound odd given the life we have led, but true never the less.

He lives, and has always lived in a town called Felling, an absolute `dodge city` of a town, I, in my time, have had a couple of bars in Felling, it is truly a crazy town, the whole place revolves around alcohol, all day long, people in the Felling are just mad on the drink. I could have mounted a camera in the corner of my bar and sold the footage to channel four as the new shameless,

I shit you not,

The people in the felling are so game that some of them even had the name of my bar tattooed on the backs of their heeds for a few pints, the place is fucking hilarious, full of character and characters but all the time looked over and policed by "Big" Billy Robinson.

Billy runs the place, it feels like he is the sheriff in a frontier town, BUT, I can't stress this strongly enough, he is respected beyond compare, you might think this is born out of fear, and if it was it would be well warranted, but it is respect.

Has Big Billy got a pedigree? fuck me yes, shot, stabbed, the lot, has he been beaten, yes he has but the person I saw beat him 'one on one' will tell you today that Billy is hard to beat and he wouldn't want a re-match, trust me, in our world, that is huge praise, Big Billy? the man, the myth, a legend in his own lifetime

I don't think I can leave Felling without mentioning two other people who I do hold a lot of respect for, the first is Jeffery Joe, on first sight of Jeffery most people say, fuck me look how big he is, and yes he is a lump, he is *VERY BIG*, as the saying goes, he stops a lot of light. Can he fight? of course he can, and does! but in the time that I knew Jeff, I was impressed at how intelligent, polite and very well dressed he is.

When I think of Jeff Joe I can't help thinking of his "party trick", let me explain, The term psychiatry is the science or the study of human behavior, this is what he is good at, and he seemed to have a uncanny knack of "weighing" people up, and predicting their next move, personally I always found him to be a gent, if you did a favor for him, he paid it back , in fact one occasion when he was being held by the cossers I loaned him a house away from Gateshead so that he would have an address he could be released to, it was hilarious when we got there, we weren't there five minutes and about twenty cossers arrived, I recon more out of curiosity than anything else, Jeff and me in the same place together, it was like they had come to see Ronnie and Reggie, there were even two cossers on pushbikes !
.

So is Jeff Joe a gangster, probably not, I don't even think he would appreciate being called a gangster, a hard man?

Definitely, yes in spades. A truly big man and a big character and definitely a "face".

Lastly I will touch on another man from Felling, Paul Ashton, a huge bear of a man, big in every way, size and rep. First let me say this, Paul has just done 17 years, in one sitting! a good deal of that as a cat A prisoner, after what only can be described as a gun fight in the street with a rival, Stuart Watson, as no one was hurt in these fun and games, the 32 years Paul got sentenced to seems a bit keen!

Paul Ashton and his pal Robert Webber were once likened to *THE KRAYS COME TO NEWCASTLE* even Charlie Bronson Britain's most notorious hard man wrote of Paul in his book, 'Paul Ashton is the most terrifying man I have ever met, would I agree? well I almost considered offering to team up with Paul, so I got to know him pretty well, I would say Paul Ashton is a man with a fantastic sense of humor but it's also highly likely he is terrifying when asked.

I often thought we seemed to be on the same wave length and normally that would be good enough reason to team up, but sadly at that particular time he (and possibly me) carried a lot of attention from the cossers so it simply did not make good sense for me at that time, but I often think what might have been.

Chapter 4
LENNY " THE GOVNOR McLEAN

O k not a Geordie but a man, so impressive that he deserves a mention in any book about the underworld

Although Lenny Mclean is clearly a London gangland figure and has, to my knowledge never lived in the Northeast, I feel that I should say a little about Lenny, or as he is affectionately known " The Govnor". How could anyone deny the legend status this man carries.

Lenny was Born in Hoxton, London, he was introduced to the gangland lifestyle by his uncle, Jimmy Spinks, and Gipsy, Kenny Mac who arranged his first bare knuckle fight (which he won by knockout). Unable to compete as a licensed boxer due to his criminal background, Lenny entered the world of unlicensed bare knuckle fighting. He was a formidable man and claimed he could beat anyone, with or without gloves. Lenny sent out various open invitations to high profile fighters of that time including Mohammed Ali and Mr "T" no less! none of these challenges were accepted.

Lenny had three brutal fights with Roy "pretty boy" Shaw, this monster (Shaw) was once a patient of Broadmoor, a true holiday camp for grade A nutters, the crack is Roy liked it in there!

Lenny lost the first fight and won the second and third fights by knockout in the first round of both fights, with Roy Shaw being launched out of the ring.

About 1986 in another bout in the ring Lenny was matched with "Mad" Gipsy Bradshaw, at Eltham, London, Lenny at this time was at his best, heavy solid and powerful, when the referee called for them to touch gloves before the fight Bradshaw nutted Lenny, so the bell rang and the first punch of the fight put Bradshaw down, but I guess because of the sly nut Bradshaw got in Lenny went berserk and set about the Gipsy on the floor, he really knocked the fuck out of him including stamping on Bradshaw more than a few times, Lenny had to be kept back by a team of big lumps to stop the punishment he was giving to the Gipsy. The fight was all over in a few seconds, that Gipsy had no business being in the ring, he was out classed, and out fought, I know, I was there!

Lenny's claim to have had over four thousand fights, and to have never been beaten on the cobbles is probably very near to the truth, feeling is he is the greatest unofficial heavyweight world champion that there has ever been.

Lenny Mclean was quite rightly known as the king of the bouncers in London, and owned his own pub, along with Charlie Kray (yep, Ron & Reggie's brother, laughingly termed the most legitimate of the three brothers) this pub was called "GuvNors" and was the haunt of the most elite of London gangland figures. Lenny also acted as a minder to celebrities and TV actors from EastEnders etc., he was also called in as a fixer to help smooth the way for many underworld deals and to ward off the attentions of the American branch of the Mafia and reportedly the provisional IRA! true? why not, to my knowledge he moved in these circles and could open many doors which were firmly closed to everyone but the elite of any society.

The best guess is that there were four attempts made on Lennie's life, he was shot on two occasions and stabbed on another two, one of these attacks were from a drug dealer Barry Walton, the crack is, Lenny later caught up with Dalton, what happened? I don't know, so I couldn't and wouldn't say, however Dalton had many enemies and had upset many underworld figures, he was later found dead with a bullet in his head! Lenny insists he has no knowledge about who committed the murder, however Lenny was arrested for the murder of Gary Humphries by superintendent Leonard "nipper" Read, the cosser famous for collering the Kray twins, Lenny insisted he was innocent and was cleared of murder by jury at the Old Bailey, Lenny Mclean? watch the film Lock stock and two smoking barrels, in which Lenny played the role of Barry the Baptist, there wasn't much acting by Lenny, he was just being Lenny!

Chapter 5

Ernie Bewick
(Sunderland)

Ernie Bewick
Sunderland

We can't talk about the North east without talking about

Sunderland, and in Sunderland the king is Ernie Bewick. Ernie rose to fame when he was involved in the murder trial of Tony Waters after a fight at the EastEnders pub in Sunderland, which ended in a death, the ins and outs of Tony Waters death are not important here, he has served a prison sentence for that matter and it is now closed.

For a considerable time, the private security industry in the Wearside area has been over seen by Ernie, there have been smaller companies set up in competition, but they don't last long. Bewick Security signs can be noticed in most pubs, takeaways and taxi offices in and around Sunderland, he runs a tight and efficient business. So the man, well as looks go, he does look the part, he has had a good reign at the top of his tree and is well known in the north east underworld.

The story goes that Viv Graham came to Sunderland to muscle in on Ernie's "doors", both men were happy to have a straightener to resolve the matter, all accounts say that the fight, although brutal was about 50/50, but no doors were lost to Viv, and let's remember a very important fact, Viv Graham was reputedly the hardest man in the north of England, have a look at his fight with Stuart Watson on You tube, Viv was no man to take lightly.

Ernie Bewick, definitely a "face"

Chapter 6
Liddle Towers
Chester le Street

I couldn't write this book without mentioning a man that is no longer with us, in fact he died in the seventies after an "episode" with Durham Constabulary, but as a pup I was involved with Liddle, he was my boxing coach, he was fucking ruthless with me, it was pain pain and more pain. Liddle Towers was one of the strongest men I have ever had a hold of, he was freakishly strong it was like hanging on to a tiger. when I was may be 14 and under his management I was matched up with an older kid from the TA in Durham, he was about three years older than me and taller, I could do nothing with this kid my ass was getting well and truly kicked, at the end of the second round Liddle was giving me the team talk, calling me fucking useless really but I had the stones to carry on so the bell rang and I had to face this lanky prick for another beating, as I walked towards him he was grinning at me, and I couldn't resist, I round house kicked him in the thigh and his leg just went dead, I chewed the tapes of my gloves and proper set about this kid, in the background I could hear the bell ding ding ding but fuck it the kid was on the mat now and his neck was clamped between my legs, and I put someone to sleep for the first time!.

I was banned from the ABA for life, Liddle thought it was a bit excessive, cheeky bastard, he taught me how to do it.

Liddle worked a couple of doors, the incognito in Houghton, and the key club in Birtley. At about 15 he had me working at the incognito with him, at that time in the 70's there was no SIA, doormen were not licensed, the only real requirement is "can you have a row".

Liddle was big loud and "handy", when I was working with him he liked violence, I mean he REALLY liked violence, in or out of the ring, it fascinated him, he often used to say to me, if you get into it tonight with the punters and lose, I'm gonna flog you too, I was 15! so good schooling? well I am what I am, Liddle was a lump who liked a row but he wasn't a bully, anyone who got into it with him and lost, deserved it.

Liddle towers died in the custody of Northumbria police, I'm sure that he was " awkward" when he was arrested I'm also sure it was more than one cosser that beat Liddle towers to death! Liddle Towers, you were a proper stand up mush, respect.

Chapter 7
THE SAYERS FAMILY (NEWCASTLE}

**John Sayers
Newcastle**

Stephen Sayers
Newcastle

One family which casts a big shadow over Newcastle is the Sayers family, the main players being John, Stephen, and Michael, are (were) they criminals and gangbangers? well let's have it right, of course their lives have included organized crime.

Johns father has in the past been shot in the neck and, Michael was shot at least six times AND LIVED!

So John, well this man is a "leg end" in the north east, on the face of it a quiet un-assuming man, which leads people to think 'can he turn it on' fuck yes, he can *pagger* with the best of them, but there are three of them, three very close violent brothers with an enviable nationwide rep, trust me, ask up and down the country about the Newcastle underworld and you will hear the name Sayers!

John Sayers hit fame when he was arrested for the murder of Freddie knights, Freddy was shot dead in a "gangland" style execution on his mother's doorstep, John was the key mush on offer for planning the murder but in a three-month trial at Leeds court he was acquitted of all charges and walked free. three other men in the same trial were convicted of man slaughter.

Seven years after the trial a known police informant, Errol Hay came forward and stated that he was instructed by John to telephone one of the jurors in the original case and threaten him, this is known as "*jury knobbelling*" or perverting the course of justice. Hay, a known police informant was immediately given the term "super grass".

The informants contract was organized by a high ranking Cps prosecutor David Kingsley Hyland, and John was back on offer for perverting the course of justice, if this had gone all the way John would almost certainly have died in prison. Of course this was lies, once again, and rightly so, John walked out of court a free man

John Sayers has, of course served some jail time, he served 15 years for the Pritchards security robbery in 1989, and another 4 for tax evasion. but anyone reading this and who knows John will also know this, to underestimate this man is fool hardy at best, he is a man of huge intelligence, and he is at the top of the career path that he decided to follow, his brothers Michael and Stephen albeit to a slightly lesser degree are in the same league as John.

The Sayers family? they are in the "top drawer" of their profession, all efforts by Northumbria Police Force both legal and illegal have had little or no effect on John and his family. It is widely known that the cossers in Newcastle even have a department dedicated to a securing a serious conviction against John Sayers, to date? it has not happened.

In another book

"THE SAYERS, TRIED AND TESTED AT THE HIGHEST

LEVEL" written by Stephen Sayers he comments that the only way he can leave his criminal past will be to leave the Uk, I agree, no matter how hard I have tried, it is in my opinion impossible if you are involved in "the life" impossible to leave your past and notoriety behind, the UK authorities won't allow that, you become a fair target for any prick a with warrant card and a small cock.

My problem was the two police forces, Durham and Northumbria, officers from both of these forces continually persecuted me in day to day life, even down to harassing my wife on the street with the fucking stupid accusations like "gangsters moll" My wife on a night out once asked a cosser for some help with some piss heads that were bothering her and her pals, his reply? where's your hard man husband? get him to help you!

come on, grow up you fucking idiots, my wife has never nicked a knicker in her life, her only "crime", is, she married a, what police term as an active gangster, of course I'm not a gangster let alone an active gangster, but let's remember we are speaking about cossers here.

One last point of note, David Kingsley Hyland, who knew that the "supergrass" agreement given to Errol Hay was in fact based on direct lies by Hay, and in my opinion suggestions by the police and CPS, but let's have it right, Errol Was a smack head and at best was as numb as a stump, so did he get "help" from the authorities with his statement.

As I said earlier, it looks like he did, and an old saying goes like this, if it walks like a duck, and it quacks like a duck, it's a fucking duck, having said this, one point is worthy of note, David Kingsley Hyland is still to this day employed as a senior prosecutor for the CPS and is under orders from his employers not to discuss this case in question with the media, of course you must draw your own conclusions on this matter, but I myself have seen corruption by police and cps at first hand, and this old "gangster" will state now, in the UK this happens a lot. Errol Hay died shortly after that case! karma can be a real bitch when she sticks it in and breaks it off!

Chapter 8
(PADDY) CONROY
(NEWCASTLE)

"Paddy" Conroy Newcastle

P addy Conroy? I like him, everyone likes him! He is a hugely likable character and in some ways a naturally funny man, he always has a smile on his face, you can't help but like him, but just like in the case of John Sayers, don't be fooled, there is a line in the song

A BOY NAMED SUE

by

Johnny Cash

and the line is this,

" he kicked like a mule, and bit like a crocodile"

So, do you get the message? true in London or Marbella he might be a bit out of his comfort zone, but in his own town, Newcastle, or the *toon*, as it's affectionately known, he is more than a force to be reckoned with!

And let's not forget, Paddy Conroy has been the UK's most wanted fugitive by the authorities and has had an underworld price put "on his head" of £100,000! but despite that, he escaped at least one hitman who attempted to lure him to a remote farm house.

Paddy has had many dealings with Northumbria police, he served a lengthy prison term along with his co-defendant David Glover for the alleged kidnapping, DIY dentistry and sundry torture of Billy Collier, member of a rival gang who, amongst other things, boasted that he intended to desecrate the grave of Paddy's Father, topped by the dramatic escape from the prison transport taxi and police custody on the Felling bypass, he did get to Spain but was collared a few months later.

Paddy spent 10 years in jail for that caper, but has always vehemently denied the crime, he even subjected himself to a lie detector test to prove his innocence, he doesn't deny he did beat up Billy Collier, but he continues to insist that he did not play any part in the torture, or the teeth pulling.

Paddy Conroy is liked in the west end of Newcastle, he is respected by many, when he was arrested for the torture of Collier along with David Glover there was nothing less than riots in the streets of Newcastle, his pal, Michael Bulloch climbed to the very top of the Tyne Bridge in protest over his arrest.

The rivalry between Paddy Conroy, the Richardsons and the Sayers family, especially John Sayers is well documented, especially by the local rag, The Evening Chronicle, sometimes it looks like that particular newspaper would go out of business if it wasn't for Paddy and John Sayers.

There is an opinion that the Sayers family, especially John Sayers gained the west end of Newcastle turf crown when Paddy spent ten years in jail, Paddy doesn't agree! a quote from Paddy when referring to John Sayers in a TV interview,

" in one breath he says he is the godfather of Newcastle, in the next breath he's in the dock coppering (grassing) every cunt",

who knows.

As I said, there is a long standing feud between Paddy and the Sayers family, local feeling is that at some point there needs to be a "straightener" between Paddy and Stephen Sayers, both have much to say about each other, all of it bad, so where does the balance of power lie, in the west end of Newcastle? who knows, but it does feel as if there is a power vacuum, but at some point there will be a king!

Chapter 9
Michael "the bull" Bulloch

(Newcastle)

Michael "The Bull" Bulloch

Paddy Conroy has a very close pal or even right hand man,

Michael *"the bull"* Bulloch, this man is adhesive with Paddy, a lifelong friend and enforcer working alongside Paddy on the doors of clubs and pubs in and around Newcastle. Michael has served a four-year jail sentence for drug related offences, he claims he was set up by Northumbria Police after being secretly filmed being handed an ounce of cannabis, this claim is defended by Paddy Conroy, who goes on to say the sentence was too harsh but " the bull" will do what he has to do, he will just get on with it.

Michael Bulloch does have a worthy underground pedigree and he is, most definitely a "face", and hard man, when asked about a crime concerning a firearm in his past, he replies

"I shot Billy Thompson, unfortunately, his legs fell off! "

Michael may never have achieved the infamy that his pal

Paddy Conroy has, but he is very much a man with a presence in Newcastle, having served his time "*on the doors*" in and around the Northeast.

Chapter 10

Ian (The Machine) Freeman

Ian
"The Machine"
Freeman

Ian is not a gangster, he is not a criminal, but he is a *face* in the northeast, and the reason he is a "face" is simply this, he is truly a hard man!

I could not write this book without mentioning him in some way, I have sparred with this man, and I have been hit many times in my life, but nothing was like being hit by Ian Freeman, let's remember that Ian Freeman was the first British UFC champion. everyone in the UK who calls themselves a "cage fighter" and lets have it right, there is a shit load who do, every one of you walk in the footsteps of Ian Freeman ! , would any of you spar with him ? , I have, it fucking hurts, and it hurts for days, he once signed a set of fight gloves for my birthday, and he wrote, from one hard man to another , true I can have, and have had many a row with people who claim to be hard men, but honestly I have never felt anything like the blows I took from Ian Freeman. so why is he in this book?

He isn't and doesn't claim to be a gang banger, criminal?

no not as far as I know,

a hard man?

The hardest.

Chapter 11

VIV GRAHAM
(Newcastle)

Of the many names that conjure up the dark flavor of the Newcastle gangster, Viv Graham has to reign supreme, sadly he is no longer with us, he was murdered on new year's eve in 1993, shot three times whilst getting into his car.

So a thug? no, not to my knowledge, in fact a close friend of Viv's, Paul "Gazza" Gasgoine said of his pal, " Viv was a gentleman gangster and had a heart of gold, he would rather help someone than hurt them" I would agree.

Viv was a very handy heavyweight amateur boxer, he entered the life working for "Big" Billy Robinson (also in this book) and another very sinister but gentlemanly gangster, Paddy Leonard, both from Felling in Gateshead. Viv ran a security firm in and around Newcastle, he looked after many 'doors' and carried a great deal of respect in the Northeast underworld,

He did have his detractors of course, very notably another doorman Stuart Watson this particular vendetta is still made famous by YouTube today, when Viv visited a club where Stuart Watson was working, Viv attacked Stuart, in the foyer, the fight was hard and very one sided, and although Stuart Watson very rightly refused to offer any evidence to the cossers, the courts used the cctv footage to prosecute Viv and he was sentenced to three years.

In his chosen trade most people will say that Viv was a very fair minded man, anyone who had to deal with the wrong side of Viv generally deserved it. Viv was very anti-drugs, he wouldn't allow anyone to deal in the venues he looked after, this brought him into conflict with a lot of dealers in the northeast, he wasn't put off and he policed his policy very hard. Many dealers tried to muscle in on Viv's patch in hope of being the main dealer, none with much success.

One person who tried to oust Viv from his door in Newcastle was Teeside hard man Lee Duffy, (also in this book), Lee made various trips to Newcastle and made an easy job out of *paggering* various bouncers working for Viv, but Lee and Viv never met to have the straightener they wanted, Lee later died in a fight with David Alison.

There is still today in the security industry country wide a sneaking admiration for the way that Viv ran his, dare I say empire? in his trade he was a true professional, he charged consultancy fees to venue owners who had problems that the police or the landlord couldn't solve, and I want to stress now, and I speak from firsthand experience, that in the pub and club trade, the police are truly worse than useless.

Viv solved problems for publicans when all else failed, and publicans were more than happy to pay for his services, I would say that Viv Graham was the first choice when venues had 'problems' to solve, often known as the as "*fourth* emergency service".

So who murdered Viv Graham? well this has to be the worst best kept secret of modern times, everyone who has an interest in this murder knows who the killer is, let's have it right, twenty years after the killing of Viv, secret police documents surfaced to show that a paid police informant disclosed to the police the name of the shooter, when asked how he knew who this, he replied, I was there, I was the driver of the getaway car ! , this informant gave a full and irrefutable account of what happened on the night Viv was murdered, the cossers took no action. even a confession to the killing from super grass Sean Lee Watson came to nothing, hmmmm, so why has the killer of Viv Graham not faced a trial? only Northumbria Police can tell us this, don't hold your breath.

Viv Graham, liked by some, hated by some, but a true "face"

Chapter 12
Raoul Moat

I gave a lot of thought to including the Raoul Moat in this book, and in doing so I in no way glamorize or condone the crimes Raoul Committed, however he did hold a place in the underworld of the Northeast and because of this I have written about my experiences with him.

There cannot be many interested people reading this book who will not have heard of Raoul Moat. Raoul is famous (or infamous) depending on your stand point, for the shooting of his ex-girlfriend, the murder of her new boyfriend, and the shooting of PC David Rathband. In the resulting standoff with armed police Raoul turned his gun on himself and that was the end of Raoul.

So what was Raoul moat like, well he was a lump, there's no doubt about that, and he was very unbalanced, again there is no doubt about that, but also he lived in a fantasy life, even though he was as Geordie as the Tyne bridge he insisted on telling people that he was trying to impress that he was French! like all pathological liars, he believed what he was saying regardless of how implausible it sounded to the rest of the world. Occasionally me and a couple of pals went fishing with him, on one of these trips we had a sort of wager, just for fun and the winner bought the beers, Raoul had a bad day, he couldn't catch anything at all, as his mood changed and his frustration grew, it became funnier and funnier for the rest of us to the point we were texting the address to him of the local fishmonger to help him out, in the end Raoul snapped, he threw all his fishing gear in the lake, called us all twats and stamped off in the huff, obviously we were helpless laughing, I could hardly breathe, he was so huffed he wouldn't even get in the car to come home, so in-between tears of laughter we told him to get fucked and left him, he walked home and didn't speak to us for weeks.

Raoul Moat spent his life in the depths of paranoia, he felt that the entire Northumbria police force went to work every day planning how to fuck up his day, he was convinced his phones were tapped, his car was tapped and his house was fitted with secret cameras, he even put his hand over his mouth when he was speaking as he thought that he was being tailed by lip readers employed by Northumbria Police!

Raoul did mix in the same circles as I did and he was involved in bit of gangland crime, along with door work and some security work. Although I can't be sure of this and it is only my thoughts, I am pretty much sure that Raoul put a lot of time and planning in to his shooting spree, I know a few days before this happened he was in touch with Stephen Sayers to ask for advice, his life was going down the pan and Stephen told him this.

Raoul was always a man in pain and I often think that even though he was a lump of a man, in his head, he was a disturbed child.

Most people I know that say the same thing about Raoul Moat, something like this was always going to happen but no one ever thought that it would be as bad as it was,

When the siege happened with Raoul, Paul Gasgoine approached Northumbra Police and asked if he could speak to Raoul and persuade him to give himself up, they refused!

For a number of years Raoul had a severe and serious hatred of Northumbria Police, he, very publically stated that the police waged an ongoing vendetta against him personally, he was obsessed with talking about this, he often hid in hedges photographing the cossers he thought were following him, most people would just laugh at this but to Raoul, it all made perfect sense.

I don't like or dislike Raoul Moat, I dislike what he did but he was always going to leave a fucking mess behind him, was he a face in the north east? at one point, yes he was

Chapter 13
John "Mario" Cummings
THE GEORDIE GODFATHER
(Newcastle)

John "Mario" Cuningham
Newcastle

John was a key player in the organization known as "The Geordie Mafia", working in the 60's his choice of crime was post offices, banks and safe cracking, John has an illustrious past in our world, so let's look at his pedigree,

The first person in 100 years to escape from Durham prison, *(he did this dressed as a woman)*

His associated with Charlie Richardson (the Richardson family of London)

Shared a prison cell with Bruce Reynolds (Great train robber)

Cell mates with Michael Luvaglio (convicted for the murder of Angus Sibbett in south hetton, in the " one armed bandit wars)

He was involved with the kray twins and their visits to Newcastle's Dolce Vita club in the 60's

John Cunningham had a long and what could only be termed as an amazing criminal career, and over 40 years reputedly stole the equivalent of millions of pounds in today's value, surprisingly, he gave most of it way to friends and family, some people likened him to a latter-day Robin Hood, or "*Robbing dude*" as he was later named.

John loved the lifestyle of the rich and famous, life was one long party to him. He likened life in Newcastle to a mini Las Vegas, and he often joked, that the movie "Goodfellas" was the story of him and his pals but with Geordie accents!

John Cunningham started his criminal life after an abusive childhood in a care home in Spennymoor County Durham, he later found himself in the Mosside area of Manchester involved in the periphery of gangland crime, he found this way of life easy and soon earned a reputation within the underworld. He soon found himself a main player both committing and planning robberies, his preference being " easy or sweet jobs" where no violence or threat of violence was needed.

He really brought a sophistication to the robberies he carried out quickly learning how to use explosives to "blow" safes, he famously had a safe from one of his jobs in his house which was used as a dining table!

John acted as a kind of consultant to many serious villains who trusted his advice when planning various capers, his attention to detail when planning his and associates jobs was obsessional, he claims that this is why he spent so little time in jail, he claims that he and his muckers were "professional" criminals, unlike a lot of the amateurs, as he says most were at that time, and he claims that this was the key to his success.

John Cummings passed away in December of 2012, the hundreds of people at his funeral a testament to the respect and reverence this man carried, not only in the Northeast but throughout the country,

John "Mario" Cummings a true "face

Chapter 14
Davey
"The beast of the Northeast"
Falcus

Davey
"The beast of the northeast"
Falcus

Ok Davey Falcus, (also known as Davey Tams) in his own words has found God, he has written his own book, *from gangland to god*, and who are we to judge?

Davey, although born in Brampton was brought up in the west end of Newcastle by step parents. after a childhood of care and borstal Davey at the age of 17 was involved in an armed siege with the police, then soon after was sent to jail for drug offences.

By his early twenties Davey was working the pubs and clubs as a doorman and was heavily involved in the Newcastle drugs scene working with the infamous Geordie Mafia, Davey says that he was a feared man in the Northeast club land, he claims he has been shot, stabbed and hit with iron bars, in my research on Davey I have read that he has mixed with the "glitterati" of underworld figures from Glasgow to London and even on the continent, Davey claims that he was the " go to man" when rival gangs wanted to meet for a straightener , there seems to be feeling that Davey was intensely addicted to alcohol and cocaine having spent more than one fortune to fund his habits.

What is clear is Davey Falcus was a very unhappy man, made worse by the life he was leading, and soon something had to "give", he looked for salvation in many religions including

Buddhism, and Hinduism but still the voices in his head urged him to take his own life. Davey says that he experienced what some people term as an epiphany, he had a meeting with God, (his words) and this what changed his life, and it was then that Jesus told him his sins were forgiven, and to sin no more, from that moment on he insists his 15-year cocaine habit and alcohol addiction disappeared for good.

Since his encounter with God Davey has been ordained as a minister of his church in Ashington , Northumberland and claims to have healed the blind, the deaf, the lame and the sick, he offers his services around the world from his website as a preacher, a healer speaker to schools, churches, and as a paid after dinner speaker at conferences, all of Davey's claims may well be true, as I don't know him I am not in a position to say otherwise, all I can say is, I have heard of this man from time to time, but I have also mixed and worked with all of the faces in the Northeast, many of these are mentioned in Davey Falcus's biography, along with crime families from Manchester, Glasgow, but I have never met Davey Falcus, not once, ever . So is what Davey has written about himself true? I simply do not know.

Davey Falcus says that he found God and the strength to leave his gangland life behind him, to choose a more spiritual and enlightened path doing good deeds for the sick and needy, if this is true, and I don't for one-minute doubt what he says because I just don't know, if it is true then this man is a much stronger man than I am.

Chapter 15
Geoffrey Harrison
NEWCASTLE

Geoffry Harrison Newcastle

There are a number of names which carry notoriety in the west end of Newcastle, names such as Conroy, Richardson, Sayers to name a few, also another family is infamous in the west end, these are the Harrisons. The Harrison brothers James Joseph and Andrew were involved in a "shoot to kill" gun battle on Westmorland road in the west end of Newcastle, these three opened fire on the Conroy's guesthouse The Happy House Hostel, but the rival clan returned fire, fuck knows how someone wasn't shot. The crack is that this was a revenge attack as the Harrisons caravan was petrol bombed earlier.

The three Harrisons thought their reputation would put anyone off giving evidence in court, but three civilians gave evidence and they were all weighed off with a cockle, (ten years). The witnesses since changed their identities and moved away from the Northeast.

The Harrisons like a war with everyone, their ongoing feud with the Conroy's has gone on for years, shootings, kidnappings, stabbings the lot, there was even talk of the Harrisons digging up Paddy Conroy's fathers body, this led to Billy Collier being kidnaped, tortured, (his front teeth pulled out with pliers) this resulted in Paddy doing over ten years, a lot of it as a cat A prisoner (for details of this see the chapter on Paddy Conroy).

But we started this chapter with Geoffrey Harrison so that's where we will end the chapter, 2004, Geoffrey Harrison was in the old Green Market, (a shopping center in the middle of Newcastle city Centre) and for reasons known only to him, he attacked some rival gang members, it turned into an all-out knife fight, and let's remember, this was in the middle of shoppers, fucking mayhem ensued, Geoffrey attacked Joe wood from behind and opened his face up with a carving knife, Robert Dunwoody joined in and he got the same, now the place is in chaos, the knife wounds didn't put these two off at all, and although they were pissin blood they got back into it with help from their pal Robert Allport, absolute fucking chaos, Geoffrey Harrison also got stabbed before the cossers arrived.

Geoffrey Harrison met his death in the same brutal way that he lived his life, he was found dead in a flat in Benwell, beaten to death with a hammer.

Chapter 16
Brian The Tax Man Cockerill

**Brian
"The Taxman"
Cockrill
Teeside**

Brian has been a prominent member of the Northeast underworld for three decades or more, if you were to see his criminal record you wouldn't automatically think "gangster" in fact it shows very little, I am led to believe it's no more than driving offences, BUT he has been arrested for attempted murder, 40+ section 18 assaults, and the attempted murder of a cosser ! and the list goes on, he has arrests for racketeering, kidnap, shootings, taxing's, firearms, but for all these arrests, Brian is innocent, because no convictions were ever successful. To a degree, my involvement with Northumbria police is similar, everything I was arrested for, I am innocent as I was never convicted. Brian may have been arrested on hundreds of occasions, but the convictions are few.

The Taxman is famous for being brutal in a fight, he claims to have had over 1000 bare knuckle fights without losing a single one, a claim very likely to be true, but his trade is "taxing" the local drug dealers in Teesside (taking their cash and valuables from them), this he did, or does? with ultra-efficiency.

Brian, whilst in this trade has been teamed up with quite a few "partners" but most notably Lee Duffy (as I wrote earlier in this book, Lee died after being stabbed in a fight with David Alison). Lee joined Brian in the taxing business after they fought each other in the street, and in Lees own words, Brian Cockrill is a man with super human strength and the ferocity of a lion!

The pair were notorious and formidable in their time, most dealers in Middlesboro just closed up shop and moved to another town rather than risk these two men kicking the front door in.

The word round the camp fire is that Brian (who is a lump of a man) would single out an active dealer who was clearly earning well and "go round to his gaff" for a chat, this involved kicking in the front door and persuading the kid in the house to part with all the cash, drugs and tom (gold and jewelry) that was in the house, if the little scamp wasn't forth coming Brian would get a violent and play the "little piggy" game, which involved the drug dealers toes and a hammer !, eventually most gave up their loot, sometimes as much as 50 grand. He says no one ever got past two toes!

So what was the dealer going to do? go to the gabbers and say his hard earned cash and drugs had been stolen, no of course not.

Brian had the franchise on this type of business on Teesside, it worked and worked well for a long time, but he did make some dangerous enemies, I don't think anyone ever thought a one on one straightener was a particularly good plan, however he was once lured to a on Teesside, when inside he was attack by, what most people agree was a gang of at least ten people tooled up with hammers and bats, Brian more then held his own, and although he feels that they were out to kill him, all the managed to do was beat him up a bit, 170 stitches, 2 pints of blood and a lengthy hospital stay, BUT, Brian walked out of the house on his own feet!, and everything said, this must be a testament to how fit and powerful this man is.

Recently Brian has been attempting to run as the mayor of Middlesboro, he claims that he, if elected, can rid the streets throughout Teesside of crime and criminals, what the gain would be to Brian I can't say, only he will know that, but I think Cleveland Constabulary and Ray Mallen might have something to say about Brian being the mayor of Middlesboro. Never the less, when speaking about Brian The taxman Cockrill you can say this,

feared? yes

respected, certainly

a face? definitely

Chapter 17
Lee Duffy
{Middlesborough}

Lee Duffy
Teeside

Athough Lee lived a little way out of our manor, Lee Duffy needs a mention in this book. Lee grew up in the Southbank area of middlebrow, he was an accomplished boxer as a youth and went on to work "on the doors", sadly he drifted into the drug trade and things went from bad to worse, along the way he made many enemies and pretenders to his throne. It's said that Lee saw himself as indestructible and one account has him playing Russian roulette with a hand gun, that's the way it is when the Charlie gets a good hold.

Lee is no longer with us, he died after a stabbing whilst in a one on one fight. Lee survived at least three attempts on his life, two shootings and an incident when a rival tried to douse him in petrol and burn him alive, this failed. Some people say that Lee Duffy was a Jekyll and Hyde character, on one hand reveling in extreme violence and on the other being a loving family man and father, even the police have been known to say that in their dealings with Lee he was polite and cooperative when arrested. So how did Lee die? at a party in Southbank Lee got into an argument with a former pal David Alison, they decided to have a straightener in the car park, after a while, Lee who was wearing a duster had the best end of the fight, and had done a good bit of damage to Alison, then someone handed Alison a knife and he stabbed Lee under the left armpit, this stopped the fight, Lee was taken to middlebrow hospital but died from his injury later that day. David Alison handed himself into the police the following day, he later faced trial for the killing of Lee Duffy but was found not guilty of all charges. Many people have tried to muscle in on Lee's turf but have not succeed, the police have been known to quote, it will be difficult for anyone to take Lee Duffy's place as crime lord of Teeside.

Finally

Newcastle and the northeast has an underworld that has long been and is still today respected by gangsters, criminals and hard men nationally and internationally, some of the most colorful gangland characters and faces have originated from the Northeast, "Panda" Anderson, Viv Graham, Mario Cummings, Billy Robinson, John Sayers, Paddy Conroy, Paul Ashton, Ted "machine gun Kelly, Dennis Stafford, Vince Landa, Paddy Leonard, etc. etc.

True, there are many more faces worthy of being named in this book but I can only write about the people who I have known or had experiences with, and this book

I could go on and on and I would love to have mentioned more faces from the Northeast but there are men and secrets I cannot and will not write about, and these secrets will go to the grave with me.

Me?, well I am a Gipsy, not an Irish Traveler or a Romanian, but a gipsy never the less, I was born in the Northeast of England and have spent my life in most parts of Ireland and the UK, but, for me, the UK is fucked, it's on its arse, I've seen the best of Britain as a wide boy, when it was good, it was good, but now, it's not worth a bottle of pop, it's full of pedophiles and mugs that think that that robbing a pound coin is a good score, I even had a some idiot in my bar telling me he was a professional thief, his thing ?

        shoplifting from fucking pound land!

So for me it's time to follow what Gipsies call the urge to roam, and my feet are itchy.

I am an International Gipsy I can and do live anywhere in the world I choose to.

I've never felt settled before now but I'm settled here under the sun, no one recognizes me here, I'm just an old English expat living in the sun, and now is the time to say I'm retired from the life, I've seen it all and I've seen enough, like I said at the beginning of this book, watch the film " sexy beast" especially the part played by

Ray Winston..............................

Will I come out of retirement? I hope I never get asked!